like a solid to a shadow

janice lobo sapigao

MW00325314

▽ ∞ ✳

▽ ∞ ✳

2017 Creative Commons BY-SA
Janice Lobo Sapigao

Timeless, Infinite Light
4799 Shattuck Ave
Oakland, CA 94609

Genograms created by William Sapigao,
Designed for print by Joel Gregory

ISBN 978-1-937421-24-3

First Edition

Printed by Bookmobile

Distributed by Small Press Distribution

timelessinfinitelight.com

maysa: for those who are quiet
with words they don't like

"I know you have seen things that you wish you hadn't. You have done things you wish you could take back. And you wonder why you were thrown into the thick of it all—why you had to suffer the way you did. And as you are sitting there alone and hurting, I wish I could put a pen in your hand and gently remind you how the world has given you poetry and now you must give it back."

"Poetry" by Lang Leav

"*If you are reading this book, there is a high probability that your heart is broken.*

It may have been caused by a death, either recent or long ago."

The Grief Recovery Handbook, John W. James and Russell Friedman

Translator's Note

The Background

*"cardiology cannot yet account
entirely for the broken heart"*

- Carl Phillips

when i was six years old, my father passed away from a heart attack.
i remember mostly the sad things—how my brother and i kept my
father up the night before his heart attack, how we asked questions
about former president bill clinton, the way the kids in the apart-
ment complex gawked at the fire truck and the ambulance that
appeared as a result of my mother's 9-1-1 call the next morning, the
trashed family bedroom the medics left, the way my father seizured
in his hospital bed and how the nurse ushered us out, when my
mother howled at me when i didn't say goodbye as we left the hospi-
tal that night, how my mother bawled sitting next to me at break-
fast the next day when we learned of his death, how i watched t.v.
because i didn't know how to look at her. there are pictures of my
six-year-old self smiling at my father's funeral—eighteen years later
and the proof of it still haunts me. i had just learned, a year earlier,
how to smile at a camera, and as de saussure would have it, i was
prompted to recognize and react to the sign appropriately.

the first time i saw a therapist in regards to grieving my father's
death was months before my college graduation. graduation is a
glorious milestone, i think my therapist said, it's no wonder you feel
this way. your grieving process was delayed, and that's okay because
now you have the support to deal with it. i think this is why i write.
to give space and time to thought work and emotions. to recover
from loss. to keep what i can't have.

i also write from a place of girlhood curiosity. whenever i asked my
mother about how she met my father, she would always tell me the
shortest stories: through friends, it's a long story, i don't remember,
not right now, janice! she somehow revealed that my father sent
her cassette tapes of spoken love letters while they courted. he
was stationed in saudi arabia for the u.s. army, she had recently
immigrated to san jose, california, america from alo-o, umingan,
pangasinan, philippines. i asked about getting the tapes so that i
could listen and my mother would tell me the shortest stories: okay,
later, i don't remember, not right now, janice! it wasn't until i told
her that i needed the tapes for what i called a school art project that
she willfully forfeited the tapes for me to listen, digitize, transcribe,
translate and share. i have written many poems and stories honoring
the life of my father. each time, i open myself to the mercy of an
audience. each time like new. each reopening a new layer of meaning.

i do not read, write or speak ilokano, yet i can understand it fluent-
ly. this type of fluency is what carries this project. for six months, i
worked with a veteran activist, al garcia, who taught me ilokano. we
were in the process of furthering this project, but i stopped our weekly
lessons when learning the language brought me too close to a family
history that i was not ready to deal with emotionally. this is the basis
of this book.

i looked to an online dictionary and the website of the ilokano stud-
ies department at the university of hawai'i at manoa as references
for the translation.

The Text

"what we write is what we need to
keep in order for it to stay"
                                    – j. cariaga sapigao

the transcribed and translated text is from a recording of my father's spoken love letters to my mother and grandparents. i translated the side b of a tape from august 1980 marked "Start here. For Papang, Mamang, My Darling + Everybody." i chose this specific side and this tape because it is the first tape i chose to listen to when i first heard my father's voice as an adult. this project is a translation from sound to text. the tape and this text has traveled many miles, passed through many minds and exists now as an imperfect translation.

i strongly recommend listening to the digitized source recordings with this text at hand: http://www.soundcloud.com/janicepinay (begin with track 1).

The Concept

"Ultratranslation—an awareness or hum or breath...moments within translation, a part of translation parting it to expose the irreducible gaps."

– Antena

it is my intention to make this draft of this transcription and ultra-translation look like it is undergoing a process of editing. the main text is in english and ilokano roman letters. the use of roman letters should tell you that it's already too late to know or to be told. verbal arts and non-written communication thrived in philippine indigenous communities long before roman writing systems dominated currency and replicated ideas and desires toward power.

there are italicized roman letters and ilokano in sound and where another possibility exists. in addition, the italicized text is my first choice of what i interpreted and typed as i heard it; the italicized, parenthetical text is where i sift through the multiple meanings that come up for me.

because my father himself imitates bureaucratic language in his speech, i understand that joining the army was one way to retain and learn english after having some schooling in the philippines.

i want to tell you what words in ilokano mean, yet i believe that it is an important political choice for me to have readers work to understand and to construct their own meanings, at the risk of feeling frustrated or failing. by posing my text, then, as a dialogue, i attempt to distort dominant frames of reference. if the reader chooses to read just the roman or parenthetical parts of the line, then either text exists to perform an impending distraction, an ignored body, to show or hide the poetics of violence, or the opportunity for poetry in the margins.

as a translator, i want my reader to have choices, options and decisions available to them. i want my translation to hold, most importantly, the feeling of an experience that is fleeting and disappointing. i want the page to appear simple and to contain what is most important to me—which is the seemingly straightforward presentation of a text and the underlying tumultuous journey that undoes it.

like a solid to a shadow

daytoy

this one
the sun around us
overcasts arrows at
mountains we forgot

katigid

to go left
stand at the edge of the cliff
move forward a bit
use your tippy toes
til you feel a string of concrete
on the balls of your feet

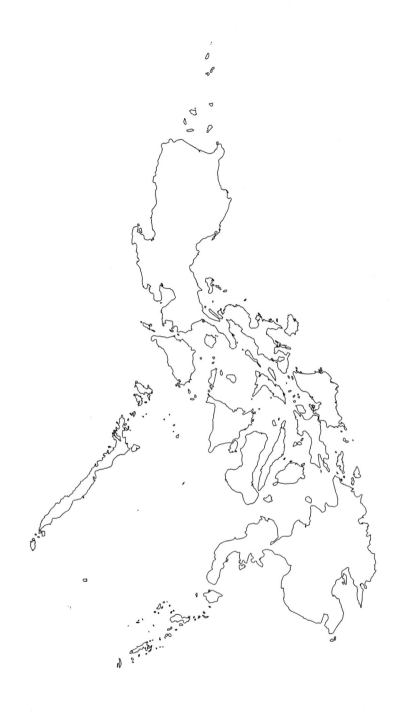

A Map of The Philippines

What broken California am I from   what x-ray lacks bone and lays
underexposed   What splints for borders make a wrestling match for
citizenship

Whose war on drug lords   of what government   What mouths like trap doors
spin a labyrinth   What revolution becomes a street sign   Isn't a line a
series of dots

What people power   What crown of thorns we are   This thorax poetry
makes foreign headlines makes the street a wake makes a sinking cruise liner of a

country Yeah   What country   just this mass of followers   born from the sword
they brought to iron a sobering laughter   Pretend I'm a package Pretend I'm
coming undone

A typhoon of knives a failed strangle Pretend the outsourced women as weapons
What weapons What sharp shouting in English this grip panel of teleseryes &
dancers

You hit & run unsolved crime collection of belly buttons you mayonnaise inside
you mayonnaise outside   You minute hand jacking   you a old teddy bear

Pretend fire Pretend I open from flame   Pretend this open flame breaks poorly
into orange   Pretend these embers catch roots   a rhizome   a rope a fist
a crack

A semi-automatic kundiman   We camouflage American   We varicose ink   We a
dinosaur ghost   What good is your compass   If you got scissors for eyelids

if you pretend Magellan   if you Columbus   What time period did you sleep on
Pretend you erase when you don't remember if you pretend you don't see us now
what?

This a shredded blindfold Not your nanay's house no more   Your paradise come
from explosive smoke Your slippers ain't armored cars Your pretending costs lives

Where My Name is From

My name is Janice. Janice Lobo Sapigao. I am from San José,
California. The Bay Area. Not quite San Francisco. Not at all
Oakland. I am from the in-between. I am from a pause, a needed
moment of clarity. I am from the face people make when I don't
answer with a birthplace of an Asian country. I am from the way
I have to justify myself when I say I was born here. I am from my
parents. My mother says my father named me.

My mother told me that my father, whose name might be John
in English, named me. His name might Juan or Jun. Juh. Juh.
The 'juh' in Janice sounds like a joke, like do you get it?, like the
unfunny punchline, like you're about to sneeze but decide not to
after all, after your fingers are clamping down your nose, and the
'niss' in Janice pretends to hide behind itself. Like you can see
its shadow, like you have to pretend it is not there. 'Janice' means
a form of Jane, which is a female form of John. 'Janice' means
'Jane' means 'John' means I come from my father whose name is
not his own.

My family says my name like this: 'Jah-neese.' The 'jah' means
agreement, means 'yeah, sure' means 'yah' means 'yeah, whatever'
and the 'neese' sounds like 'look here, I found you, in that spot,
called ni! I see you there, your shadow tells me, ni-esss, neese, my
daughter, my girl relative, my niece, you are not hiding, for why are
you hiding?, come out."

I am Ilokana. My mother is from Alo-O, Umingan, Pangasinan,
Philippines. My father is from Asingan, Pangasinan, Philippines.
My stepfather is from Cabugao, Ilocos Sur, Philippines. Umingan,
Asingan, Cabugao, Pangasinan, Philippines, when translated into
English, it means 'very far.' It means 'hella far.' It means your
tongue and your stomach must get used to being off the grid, to

bumpy roads and potholes made bigger by monsoons and tsunamis. To far monsoons and far tsunamis that are caused by the drought called homesickness. To homesickness as flight. To homesickness as a poetic curse. To homesickness as the route on the map. To the end of 'far' as the end of homesickness.

My name 'Janice' does not exist in Filipino. Janice is Janeese is non-existent in the Filipino alphabet, called Baybayin. The 'J' (juh) sound and the rule 'I before E except after C'—the rule whereby my name is exemplified—and the 'C' as an 'S' (C is 'cuh' and 'S' is 'essss', not 'C' as 'essss') further complicates the location of my name. My name, therefore, is very much American, very much English. My American name overshadows where I am from.

My middle name 'Lobo' means wolf in Spanish, means 'balloon' in Filipino, means 'embarrassing' in middle school when my friends find out. 'Lobo' depending on how you pronounce can also be read as 'lubo' or 'lubong' which is mud, or earth, or the globe. My middle name is place and I return to it. It is an in-between. 'Lobo' to me, sounds like no, no, don't go there, this is rock bottom, this is the end, but the end won't end. This is a poem.

My last name Sapigao means 'wait until you're 24 to do enough research, to ask questions, to wait and to find out that it only means 'nuts.' 'Nuts of the bird.' Sapigao means 'pretend it means seeds, seeds of a bird.' Then poeticize the bird, let it fly. Then poeticize the seeds, 'I am the seed of a bird that flies.' My dad flies. My dad is the bird. I carry his name far. I fly.

Notes from Ilokano Lesson
Language History

1. Say every sound and letter.

2. This is not about speed, this is about learning and speaking.

3. Know every word.

4. Remember that Ilokano is a foreign language.
5. It is written as you hear it.
6. Test sounds with your ear.
7. There are old words, new words, dying words.

There exists in the world pictures of my father as a worker in Saudi Arabia. I think he was in the U.S. Military. I think he was an engineer. I think he was holding a gun. I think he was topless, showing off his numbered tattoos. I think he was sitting in a bunk with a yellow-orange blanket. I think he was smoking. I think he was with my mother at the time. I think he was is my father.

He was is in the picture.

He was is.

I remember it.

Conversation started July 12, 2012

Gem ▮▮▮▮▮▮▮▮▮▮   7/12, 2:28pm
hello....

———————————————— August 20, 2012 ————————————————

Janice Sapigao   8/28, 12:38pm
Hi Gem,

I am sorry that I did not call you or contact you sooner.
Please let me know what I can ask my mom for you. I will
talk to her soon.

Janice

✓ Seen Sep 1

A part of this conversation is missing.

I swear that Gem, who might be one of my cousins, sent
me a message about wanting to talk to my mother, whom
I was upset with at the time he messaged me.

I swear that Gem asked for my mother's contact informa-
tion and needed it right away. I could sense the urgency,
but I did not act in like manner.

I was too upset with my mom and a bit frightened at fam-
ily members' accessibility to make contact with me.

insan

cousin (slang)
part of the family
roped together
attached by heart

looking up again

i wonder if
my father sits up there
sinking into pillows
finally
without chest pains
i wonder if
his eyes sit
on the crown of my head
on my dark brown hair
glued in anticipation

i wonder if
he chews on
the food we leave for him
on the altar
on holidays and anniversaries

Manolo
Mazie
Eliza
Blanca
Mayong
Anton
Doking
Richard
Marlena
Mazie
Cherry-lynn
Marvin
Jason
Julianne
April

i wonder if
he searches down
the same way
i look up.
wondering.

i wonder if
i make him proud
~~seventeen~~ ~~eighteen~~ ~~nineteen~~
~~twenty~~ twenty-one years
after
he had me

i wonder if he calls
lola, lola, and marlene to watch
earthen events
like graduations, weddings
and when i write

pangit

ugly
like calling out to father
where the 'n' and 'g' collide
finding that he is not there

mapukaw

lost
how it's your fault
the stolen gelatin slides
onto your tongue
and waterparks its way down
to a memory

*"No idea can construct an experience; an
experience is only lived, and its representation
endows it with a second examined life (which is
why, as it lives in the reading, it is meaningful).
The feelings of course have essentially no
language, but their ghosts haunt our words."*

Gemino Abad

The words sounds like running into a wall or the sound of almost breaking through glass or the rotund shape that's made while jumping onto a trampoline. Pangit. I think about that. Pangit. I think of how each phoneme and allophone is an element of story. I often wondered, what is a word? Is it the sound? Is it the spelling? Is it its definition? What signifies a word? Learning Ilokano felt very much like unlearning the standards of English. Writing is my attempt at healing from the delayed loss and grieving of my father and it is simultaneously an act of decolonizing and humanizing.

The experience of learning Ilokano when learning Tagalog is the preferred method of transmission for Filipina/o/x Americans (and Filipina/o/x American students) is to conjure, call out, and problematize a linguistic hierarchy. Learning Ilokano has been about learning boundaries and the realities of absence. How has the death of a father figure enacted an afterlife for (self)-discovery? How does that narrative shape or disrupt the form of a story? What forms do they take? Is Ilokano my found language?

- Spanish words and ideas entered the language, too.
- Language is development, dynamic and composed of ~~different~~ different languages.
- Language is flexible, you will learn as you go.
- Be a good speller.
- Learning Ilokano is a re-examination of English.
- It is a secondary dialect in the ~~Pacific~~ Philippines for Filipinas/o/x in the US.
- There are spoken and not written words.
- Use Baybayin for Ilokano
- Filipino languages are part of the Austropolynesian languages.
- We share common terms with Chinese and Indian languages.
- We are island people.

Tell me I didn't make it up.

Tell me that it was is real.

Tell me that he was is real.

Tell me that these pictures happened.

Can someone verify for me the truth I seek?

Can someone confirm that my hypotheses are grounded not in family rumors or hearsay, but in knowledge and witness?

Can you see the picture?

I only responded because I had seen on Gem's Facebook profile many people expressing in Ilokano condolences and aches for his life. They presented me disbelief that Gem was gone. That Gem had passed away unexpectedly.

The message I sent was an attempt to make up for the fact that I had ignored his previous messages. I thought that if I'd replied he'd reply, too. I thought that I had misread the comments in Ilokano. I suddenly wanted to converse with him knowing I couldn't.

What if the reason Gem messaged me correlated to his need to talk with my mother? ~~What if it was my fault?~~

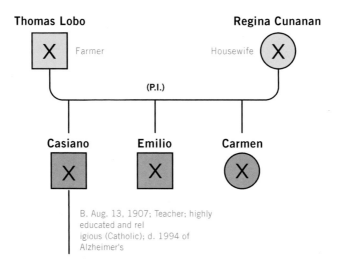

Thomas Lobo

X   Farmer

Regina Cunanan

Housewife   X

(P.I.)

Casiano

X

B. Aug. 13, 1907; Teacher; highly educated and rel igious (Catholic); d. 1994 of Alzheimer's

Emilio

X

Carmen

X

Key.

		X	Dead
P.I.	Philippines, Philipine Islands	**d.**	died, died of, cause of death
SF	San Francisco, CA	**?**	unknown information
SJ	San José, CA	**m**	miscarriage
M	Milpitas, CA	**( )**	geographic location
RC	Redwood City, CA	**B. / b.**	born
CARM	Carmichael, CA		

natay

dead, casualty
they were right here
this space
and they left

Marlena
Grandpa Casiano
Dad
Grandma Lourdes
Grandpa Alfredo
Uncle Rooney
Gary's Mom
Gary
Uncle Lito
Doking

I told a room full of Filipina/o/x and Filipina/o/x American listeners that my manuscript was about 'other' families. I think 'other families' are those that are a part of a larger one, but are forgotten about, rendered invisible, not talked about, or not known.

"The Other" is a reference to Jacques Lacan's terminology, which describes the mirror stage of development. This is the stage in growth during which children supposedly learn their own identity by successfully separating their own being from a mirror image of themselves. In this context, someone only finds an idea of themselves through a contrast with an "Other."

I think I am a part of the Other family.

Side B Track 1

play ▶   0:00-1:14

I meant to say March 22nd, and not July 22nd. It was a small mis-take made out of excitement, so mind it, and then don't mind it at the same time.

play ▶   1:15-2:04

I continued my tapings from Side A onto Side B. There's only a little bit left to say, but I don't know for sure about the duration of what I have to say, and if there's enough time to say it, because uh, I've been busy. Busy-busy. And I wished he could have called you sooner but there are two Somalian engineers with me here in the Material and Planning office. But, three. So, I took the advantage to call you after because there was a telephone, international telephone there play ▶   2:05-4:00

Dear, there's a package I am carrying and sending. Dear, I am going
to do whatever it takes to go through the hard task, of getting it to
you to register. Tomorrow, later, this will pass through the post office.
Dear, uh, maybe I should call you instead, love, I wake up and think
about you. I wanted to write to you, tell you about my day, how it is
over here, and how that's how it is, this for the affidavit of support.
About the application for visa and filling it up, which I sent to you,
to only to see, uh, the, uh, criteria of the application. So, I hope you
will understand, and, uh pray for my fast expediting to facilitate my
papers to coming there. Dear, I cannot wait to get to you because
it is my chance and opportunity, not that I am running, but I would
like to fulfill my promises to be with you. Every now and then.

NPRC.Vetrecs@nara.gov

to me ▾

Please do not respond to the following message. This message has been auto-generated by NPRC.

Thank you for submitting a request to the National Personnel Records Center.

We have received your signature authorization for request number 2-18849388575.

The record needed to answer your inquiry is not in our files. If the record were here on July 12, 1973, it would have been in the area that suffered the most damage in the fire on that date and may have been destroyed. The fire destroyed the major portion of records of Army military personel for the period 1912 through 1959, and records of Air Force personnel with surnames Hubbard through Z for the period 1947 through 1963. Fortunately, there are alternate records sources that often contain information which can be used to reconstruct service record data lost in the fire; however, complete records cannot be reconstructed.

We are mailing you NA Form 13075 (or NA Form 13055) which asks for additional information concerning the veterans' military service. Please use this form to provide us with as much information as you are able. This information will be used by our staff to help reconstruct service record data lost in the fire.

The form will be mailed to you within the next 24 hours.

Thank you.

End of auto-generated message

Who will fill me in?

Who will tell me what happened to my father?

What if there are no records?

Do records make someone exist?

If every woman has a grave deep inside her,

Then mine is my father's
A four-cornered stone that holds my focus
My last name etched in cement

Sapigao is not just a surname
It is the X on a map
Marking the territory of my father's body in the cemetery

Every Father's Day I follow it
This is where I celebrate
Every November for his birthday,
Every March when I can remember,
Where each visit is a prayer

A reminder that I am small against landscape
Standing above someone standing above me
My father is the bouquet of roses
Lillies, baby's breath, the occasional potted plant

They say flowers are the scent of the dead

A potent temporary reminder

I have learned to love him

By discovery

lukat

to open
padlocked poetry
peel the doors
see bottomless shelves
of word combinations

sarita

to speak
even the force of music
must be small before
it is mighty in crescendo

[Track One]

This is the continuation of my tapings from 'side A' to 'side B.' In the first place, uh, I would like to elaborate to you or inform you that, uh, in the second to the last paragraph of my tapings, there was a… a wordings there which I stated March twenty-two. Requesting an amendments, instead of July twenty-two, I stated there March twenty-two. So, to correct, despite the uh, mistakes, please understand, uh, na lang, dahil, uh, maybe I was so excited, my, uh, my tapings. So, thereafter, uh, I request for an amendments amending the, uh, mistakes there are.

Ket, uh, daytoy, uh, tapings ko ti Side B. Uh, *As it is, there is only a little bit… so that's how it is. I don't know and I'm not sure about the* duration na because of the, uh, the busy… busy-busy. Uh, *right now, I wish I could call you but there are two* Somalian engineers *with me here in* the Material and Planning office. Pero, three, so I, took the advantage to call you after because there was a telephone, international telephone there at.

Ket, uh, *later on there is*…uh…*I have with me (I am carrying with me), over here,* a package. Ket, uh, *I am going to do whatever it takes (going to go through the hard task) of getting it to you to* register. *Tomorrow, tomorrow (later, later),* di toy, di toy, will pass by through the post office. Ket, uh, *or maybe I should rather call you (I also name you),* mahal, *I wake up and think about you.* Nag-surat *to you, tell you about my day, how it is over here,* kasta mut, uh, uh… affidavit of support ko ti pawit mo. Ti, uh, application for visa filling up, which I sent to you, uh, to…to only to see, uh, the, uh criteria of the application. So, I hope, you will understand and, uh, pray for my, uh, fast, uh…expend-, ex, ex-uh, ex-uh, expedite for, uh, the facilities… facilitate of my papers to coming there. Ket, *I cannot wait until I get there to you (I will arrive over there to you soon)* because it is my chance and opportunity, not that I am running, but, uh, I'm only, uh, I would like to fulfill, uh, my promises to be with you. Every now and then.

- The Arabians spread Islam in The Southern Philippines.
- How we count in the US is how we count in the Philippines.
- 2,000 borrowed words come from Indian languages.
- Ilokano is called "a language without Rules" by foreign learners.
- Why do people learn other languages?
- The Spanish used language to divide and conquer in the Philippines.
- Spanish was the language of the elite.
- They did not formally teach it to the Filipinos.
- Filipinos learned Spanish through commerce.
- Spanish words entered by shortening numbers.

Genogram Notes

S.	Sapigao
L.	Lobo
R.	Roxx
E.	Espiritu
Y.	Yee
N.	Nogal
P.	Petines
A.	Agullana

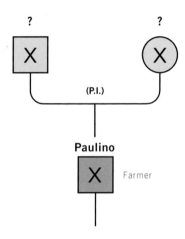

Unless otherwise stated, all members in
lineage are Filipino/Filipino-American

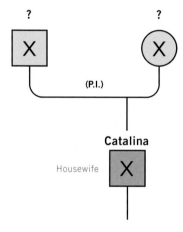

madiak

hella don't like it
you were with it until
a stray slapped you into
an uncomfortable plan b

manok

chicken
a launching guffaw
aimed at sunset
awakening the province
after indigo finishes
its shift

What happens when you do not know your family?

What happens when you discover a family secret?

If you are the family secret?

If everyone knows and you do not?

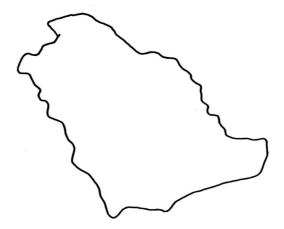

A colleague of mine told me that he used to draw
Saudi Arabia on his tests in school.

He said that his drawings reminded him of his father's
sacrifices for their family.

My partner's father lived and worked in Saudi Arabia
for sixteen years.

I didn't tell them that I refused to see it on a map.

I imagine their fatherlessness just as I imagine my own.

Apostrophize

> **Rule 1.** Use the apostrophe to show possession. To show posses-
> sion with a singular noun, add an apostrophe plus the letter s.

Example: Father's sacrifices

An example of this is "father's sacrifices." This means that the
sacrifices belong to the father. This means that he has given up,
offered – strategically, religiously, constantly. This means that he
left and that his absence is a sacrifice. That when he sacrificed
to go away, that I have sacrificed, too, because he did, because I
come from him, but you don't see that in the example. You don't
see me there. I inherited his sacrifice. I duplicate sacrifice.

Rule 2. Use the apostrophe to show the omission of letters. Apostrophes are used in contractions. A contraction is a word (or set of numbers) in which one or more letters (or numbers) have been omitted. The apostrophe shows this omission. Contractions are common in speaking and in informal writing. To use an apostrophe to create a contraction, place an apostrophe where the omitted letter(s) would go.

An example of this is "father's sacrifices." This means that, without the apostrophe, one would also be saying "father is sacrifices." The father, singular, has sacrificed many times, in the plural form. This means that more than one sacrifice has been made. That the father is an embodiment of multiple forms of sacrifice.

basa

to read
eyes mingle with each word
dating and contemplating meetings
to extract meaning from matching
at the suitor's pace

awanen

gone, passed
ma's screams clear phlegm
from her lungs and throat
from trying to flood the atriums
where she held doddy

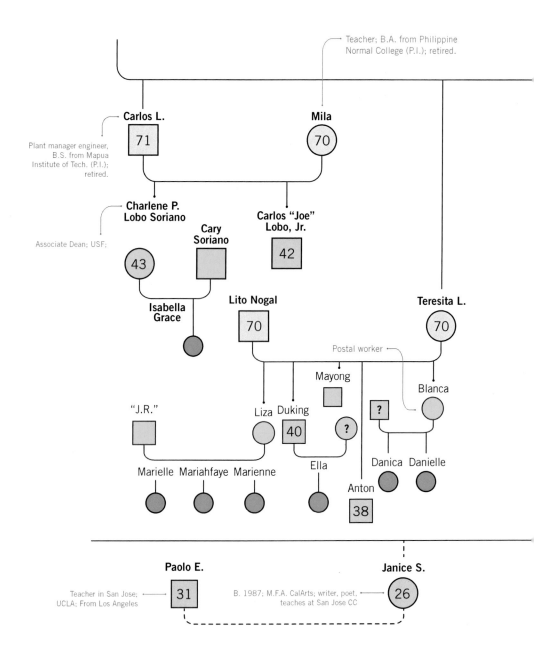

Teacher; B.A. from Philippine Normal College (P.I.); retired.

Carlos L.
71

Mila
70

Plant manager engineer, B.S. from Mapua Institute of Tech. (P.I.); retired.

Charlene P. Lobo Soriano

Cary Soriano

Carlos "Joe" Lobo, Jr.
42

Associate Dean; USF;

43

Isabella Grace

Lito Nogal
70

Teresita L.
70

Postal worker

Mayong

Blanca

"J.R."

Liza

Duking
40

?

?

Danica Danielle

Marielle Mariahfaye Marienne

Ella

Anton
38

Paolo E.
31

Janice S.
26

Teacher in San Jose; UCLA; From Los Angeles

B. 1987; M.F.A. CalArts; writer, poet, teaches at San Jose CC

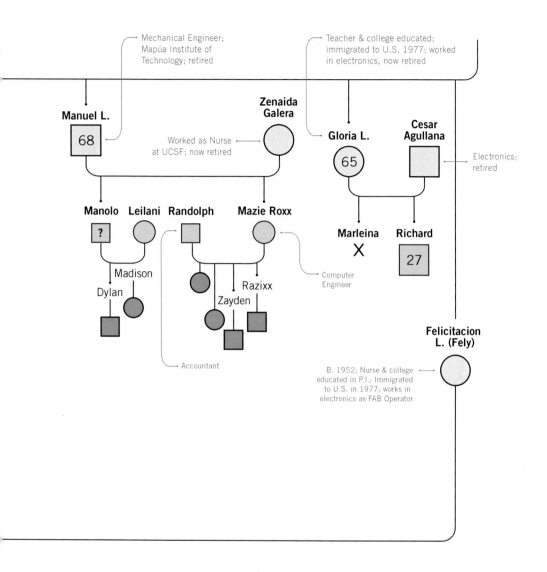

Mechanical Engineer;
Mapúa Institute of
Technology; retired

Teacher & college educated;
immigrated to U.S. 1977; worked
in electronics, now retired

Zenaida
Galera

Manuel L.

68

Worked as Nurse
at UCSF; now retired

Gloria L.

Cesar
Agullana

65

Electronics;
retired

Manolo Leilani Randolph Mazie Roxx

?

Marleina
X

Richard

27

Computer
Engineer

Madison

Dylan

Razixx

Zayden

Felicitacion
L. (Fely)

Accountant

B. 1952; Nurse & college
educated in P.I.; Immigrated
to U.S. in 1977; works in
electronics as FAB Operator

59

I was 23 years old when my mom told me that my dad used to send her spoken love letter cassette tapes.

He would speak his letters onto a microphone, which recorded onto a cassette tape.

She said she'd only listen to them once and then put them away.

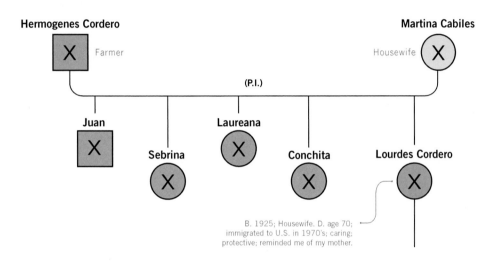

Hermogenes Cordero Farmer

Martina Cabiles Housewife

(P.I.)

Juan

Sebrina

Laureana

Conchita

Lourdes Cordero

B. 1925; Housewife. D. age 70; immigrated to U.S. in 1970's; caring; protective; reminded me of my mother.

When I get there, I have a ritual
Wipe the face of the tombstone clean
Swipe away the ants that trace the crevice of each letter
Trim the inches of tall grass that tell of our mutual absence
Cut the stems of flowers
Twist and fit them into the vase of the grave as my offer
Remember that I am at the altar of my father

Then, stand back, see how I am dotted against sky
Open mind, say something
See your work and God's
Tell him everything

That I can't wait to meet him one day
That I graduated from high school and college
That my birthday passed
That every year, I wish he could have been there
Like the last

I think that if you look at me
You probably can't tell

Mourning after nineteen years feels
Like being buried alive

Like underneath me
At the cemetery
Is the history
I'll never know,
The answers
to question that may
never have grown
had he lived.

Ana ███████████   3/13, 8:54pm

are you the son of john sapigao ?
i saw you when you were a little kid maybe 2 yrs. old. but
that was a long long time ago. i am sure you dont know
me but maybe you heard about my name. i have another
sister her name is marjorie.

i just thought of you and your sister bec. today is my
father's b-day and also the other was his death
anniversary.

God Bless!

—————————————— March 17, 2011 ——————————————

 Will Sapigao   3/17, 12:35am

Yes, John Sapigao was my father. I don't remember you
or your sister but my mother may know. How are you
related to my father, John?

Seen Sep 1

gapputa

because
the object on the table
exists because
we gave it life and power

nakem

emotions
the shield you carry
penetrable only by
piercing intangibles

This is the same person:

My dad

My Father

Son

This man   on the   tapes

Juan C. Sapigao

Juan Sapicao

John Sapiago

stranger

John Sapigao   a man in love

Johnny

Juan Cariaga Sapigao

parent

Johnny C. Sapigao

the deceased

immigrant

Juan Sapigao, Capt. U.S. Army

J. Sapigoa

"Doddy"

mahal

Uncle

SAPIGAO, U.S. Army

I told my mom that I needed the tapes for an art
project for a class I was taking.

I decided that I would attempt to transcribe and
translate the tapes for Jen Hofer's 'Poetics of Trans-
lation' course in graduate school, with what large
and little I knew about Ilokano.

I can fluently understand and directly translate
words spoken in Ilokano.

However, I cannot read or write in the language.

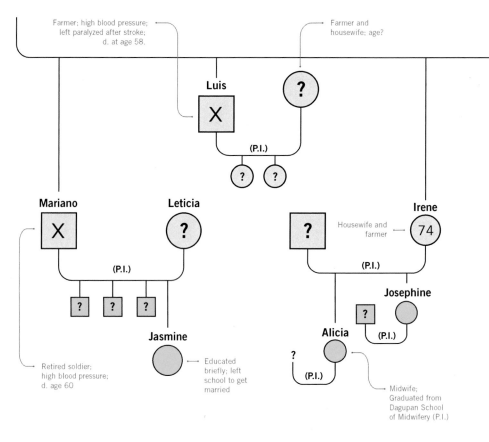

Farmer; high blood pressure;
left paralyzed after stroke;
d. at age 58.

Farmer and
housewife; age?

Luis

X

?

(P.I.)

? ?

Mariano

X

Leticia

?

Irene

Housewife and
farmer

74

(P.I.)

?

(P.I.)

Josephine

? ? ?

?

Jasmine

Retired soldier;
high blood pressure;
d. age 60

Educated
briefly; left
school to get
married

Alicia

?

(P.I.)

(P.I.)

Midwife;
Graduated from
Dagupan School
of Midwifery (P.I.)

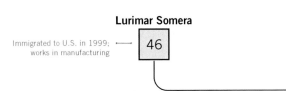

Lurimar Somera

Immigrated to U.S. in 1999;
works in manufacturing

46

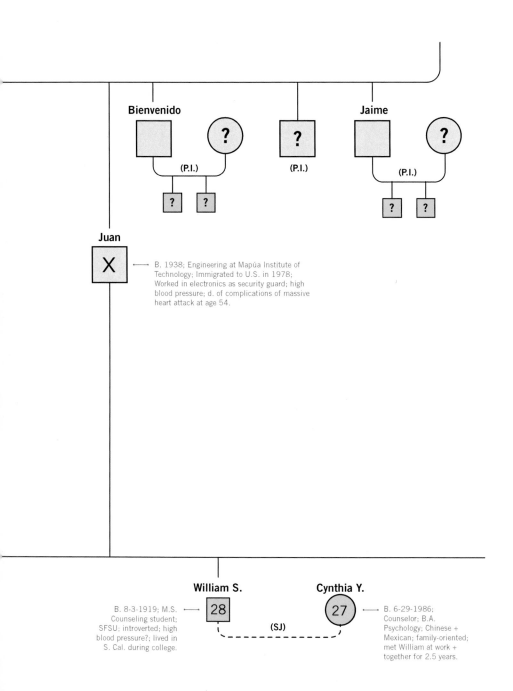

Bienvenido

(P.I.)

(P.I.)

Jaime

(P.I.)

Juan

X ⟵ B. 1938; Engineering at Mapúa Institute of Technology; Immigrated to U.S. in 1978; Worked in electronics as security guard; high blood pressure; d. of complications of massive heart attack at age 54.

William S.

B. 8-3-1919; M.S. ⟶ 28
Counseling student;
SFSU; introverted; high
blood pressure?; lived in
S. Cal. during college.

(SJ)

Cynthia Y.

27 ⟵ B. 6-29-1986;
Counselor; B.A.
Psychology; Chinese +
Mexican; family-oriented;
met William at work +
together for 2.5 years.

ragsak

happy
difficult to come by
definitive feeling
enjoyed its closed experience

rugi

begin
the line you drag across the paper
fumbles over itself; from a cloak somewhere
and nowhere at the same time

Ana 3/17, 1:40am

I am johns Sapigao's daughter. He was married before he married your mom Fely. My sister Marjorie witnessed everything happened. It was fast and we moved on. I just thought of you and your sister Janice bec. I went to my father's grave yesterday. We have another brother and his name is Joe. He lives in Davao, Phils. When I came in California 22 yrs. Ago. He used to pick me up at my work and you & your sister were in the car. I live in the Bay Area for a long time. I live in the peninsula (actually just got moved from San Jose).
Anyways, I am your older half sister!

Ana

Ana 3/17, 1:40am

It was past! Not fast! Just got home.

📱 Sent from Mobile

tanga

stupid
i threw a stone at you
it bounced off your head
you noticed tomorrow

ngato

up, upstairs
the air near your face
must ascend
make your eyes higher
above you

No trace, no sound
No trail
Just a dead end
Where my father sleeps
Like his spirit is dormant within me
And no conjuration
No evocation
No prolonged period of crying could resurrect him

My family is not whole, just a fraction
A slice of a shadow of where he should be
I say I'm from a family of four with one missing
If every woman has a grave deep inside her,
Then mine is my father's
Where cardiology cannot yet account
For the broken heart
Where heart attacks leave little room for healing
Where healing is a process

You probably don't know what you're doing. You might think you have a handle on things, might think yourself tough, smart, sweet, challenged. Really, though, you're cozy, comfortable, into the telling of the project instead of the telling of the story.

You write from an unapologetic standpoint. This isn't wrong or bad or negative. You just do. You know this story - the one that sits inside you - and you have to give it the space to breathe and live. It's what you want from your father.

Who says you need to be capable? Ability will come from trying, showing, learning, educating, working. Ability is there. Ability is stretching yourself and "going there" and coming back to tell it like it is.

You think it's difficult to keep discovering, but it's what you're doing. Exploring. Discovery is a process of struggle, hustle, and poetic motion, if you let it. If you look back, look up, look forward. So, of course, this project will be difficult. But you are able. And you've been searching. Will you find anything? You don't think you will. You think you already know the end result: that no matter how hard you try, he won't come back. He can't. That's the reality. But you can conjure up a spirit. You believe in spirits. But you don't want to conjure up a spirit.

When I asked my mom if I could have the tapes,
she said yes.

She had them ready for me at her house when I
came to pick them up.

Ti abugida nga Iloko.

a	e/i	o/u	ka	ga	nga

ta	da	na	pa	ba	ma

ya	la	wa	sa	ha

a ba ka da e ga ha i la ma na o pa ra sa ta u wa ya

Try making up some of your own words using different syllable combinations:

_____

_____

_____

_____

_____

_____

My father is still alive. I carry him because I carry his last name. I see him in my brother. I don't know what he would have been like, but I know that my brother is a good man. It must be hard for my brother. To be the living legacy of a man who left before his boyhood. I wonder where my dad lives in him.

My dad lives in my throat. He's this ball of tremors, of knotted saliva that never rises, never gets coughed out. Whenever I talk about him, or this project. I try to do it smoothly. As if the bumps are not there. As if the bumps never existed. I try to talk as if I knew the words to this language that wouldn't make me cry. As if this panging blockade in my throat would break with tears, but it only gets bigger.

People say that when you tell a painful story so many times, you get used to it and it comes out easier. Mine never comes easy. Mine enlarges with each utterance and attempt. Mine is still here. As if I have swallowed my father after he left and now I can't get him to come back. He appears this way even when I try not to say something that has already triggered tears. He comes to me this way, to say or share in the moment, but not without a complete thinking-through of the consequences.

People say they empathize. When I meet people like me who've lost their fathers, I like to think we share a special bond. A twisted one that occurs after we realize that we've shared something similar. A deep pain. A deep pain that we can't explain because the language of being in the moment around it depends on a future that hasn't yet happened.

buntog

too slow
like the banana slug
who cannot play
hide and seek
as well as
she thinks
or my brother who sleeps
counterclockwise

taray

to run
sit back in the blocks
bottoms up until bullets
propel you onto the track

I kept a portable stereo in my room.

I called my friend Lorenz to stay on the phone with me before I played the first tape.

He suggested that I clear a space for my dad, in case he wanted to show up. I did. I think he did.

Contrastify

---

but[1] | bət |

conjunction

1.   used to introduce something contrasting with what has
      already been mentioned.

Example: But, I am John Sapigao's daughter.

Perhaps I am the contrast. Maybe I highlight a difference—a change
in pattern—in what was supposed to be here—in my family. 'But'
is blunt. It is punctuating, and just as it conjoins sentences, it
also declares a break in flow. 'But' serves as an interruption—the
certainty to an almost—like a solid to a shadow. It is there to point
out—to make lucid—what is seen yet perhaps not pointed out. 'But'
confirms distinction, difference.

---

2.   [with negative or in questions] used to indicate the
      impossibility of anything other than what is being stated

---

Example: But, I am John Sapigao's daughter.

It's impossible for anyone else to be me.

adda

it's there
a leap from lost to found
process of searching
using mouth (not eyes) first

sanger

to lean on
your tilting head
touches my shoulder
softly   like books
on the shelf

I played his voice over and over.

I heard him laugh, and then I realized that I had never heard him laugh before.

I pressed rewind. And then play.

I pressed rewind. And then play.

I pressed rewind. And then play.

I pressed rewind. And then

[Track Two]

This is, uh, the, uh, second portion of "Side B." Uh, mamang and papang, my, uh, beloved darling, uh, for your information, I have just arrived from, uh, the job site. So, I took advantage again to continue. The, uh, tapings which I supposed to be mailed but Im just waiting the arrival of the package so that you will be informed enough that I had already received. But, uh, due to, uh, the delayed, I just mailed this tapings and I will just write you a letter, uh, na lang. *Because there is a package waiting there (somewhere out there)*. So, therefore, I must have to go to conclusion. Before signing off, I should have to make, uh, some elaboration. And, uh, maysa pay iya. *There is (I know somewhere there exists)* a form, mahal. *If you could get (grab) that, I can fill it out over here.* Uh, *by and by, it might take a while to make full (to put my hold on it).* Uh, uh, saan ma delay, *until there is what I want, there is not a... theres is no.... theres is no...*magastos ti kayat *coming from me. And so it is (and later on there will be)* uh, adan to, *keep your eyes out (keep looking for) the chance to get out of here (this place, this here place)* the Kingdom of Saudi Arabia. Ket, uh, *there is a choosing (a picking between things) that I think I want (would like).* Ken, uh, sapay ko ma ita, *there is a big something that I want that is heavy (feels heavy, feels too big to ask or hold) because it is so far from that bottom that I find myself in. Come here, take my invitation.* Ket, uh, *I hope you pick me between all things. I don't want to be left behind (forgotten, left in the dark)....* By next week, I might be calling you again through overseas telephone call to inform you the, uh, results of my papers – which I always followed up. So, I am waiting, also the, uh, application of my visa – which I had send you. And the, uh, affidavit of support. So that you have seen, you could, uh, send that immediately because, uh, the consular office, uh, will, uh, ask me the affidavit of support despite the cash amount – which I have on hand. *So that's how it is (that's what's left there to do)* the affidavit of support. Uh, kailangan the affidavit of support, *that's what they said.*

Ket, uh, ita, I will be signing off, mahal. So because of the delayed arrival of the package – which you had sent to me, I will just inform you later on. Ket, uh, *I don't have much left to say to you (much left to write to you)*. Ket, uh, *there's a body of something heavy here (something that weighs a lot)*, fervent prayers ko. *There's that picking between things feeling again.* Kasta mut. Papang and mamang, *there's a lot here that rubs me differently (requires time to flesh out, needs a lot more thinking about)*. Ket, uh, *I will talk to you as I can, as the time allows for it, I hope that time passes here quickly so that I can.* Ket, uh, *bring me around with you, I hope you pick me (I hope you actively choose me to go with you). Make sure not to leave behind what I write (what you write). Because what we write is what we need to keep in order for it stay (so it doesn't fly away, to keep it from flying with the wind, to have it so that it doesn't become flight or wind), so it doesn't go far away from us.* So, I hope you will understand, mahal, the situation, and, uh, please understand all my shortcomings. Whatever or wherever I am. So, accept my love, my sweet kisses, my dreams, my sweet dreams, and uh.... and my fervent prayers. So, from here, I love you. I love you again. My, uh, my mahal, with all my heart, til death do us part.

sabali

other (one)
turn over the leaf
of the palm of your hand
meet your answer there

saanpay

not yet
travel on a concrete road
from the town to the barrio
even jeepneys trip

You sit your brother down on the couch. You tell him that you have something important to share, that he needs to sit down. He sits with his laptop in front of him, and you see the glare of a bright screen reflected onto his brown face making him appear lighter than it usually is.

You ask him if he's ready, to which he replies with a deep breath and a firm "yes. Okay."

You tell him what you know, "I don't know how to tell you this…but I think Doddy had another family."

You explain how you are learning Ilokano, how you have a teacher who told you that what you just revealed is so – that you asked your mother about it and it turned into a confrontation. The confrontation confirmed for you your suspicions turned truths.

You asked her what you knew, "Did Doddy have another family?" to which she replied with a deep breath and no answer. You tell your brother that she walked away from you, as usual when conversations become too hard for her and you both.

Your brother replies further, "Well…I don't know how to tell you this, but… I already knew that."

He apologizes. He says the word "sorry" over and over again. You cry. He explains how he meant to tell you in 2010, two years before this moment, when he found out – when you all still lived in the same house – but he couldn't figure out how to do it. He talks about a Facebook message with your "sister," which became a Facebook conversation, which became a secret. What's the genogram of a secret? Can you trace it back. But how many generations small is it? How many conversations big? You understand why he didn't tell you, but you didn't say it. You know now that your whole family knew, but they didn't tell you. You do not know. You keep a secret.

You cry. And cry. And cry. And

liday

sad
the moment when
you believe your lips,
how the sap elongates
thins itself into letting go

wayawaya

freedom
a power of you
squeezed between skin and nail
kicking itself into flight

"Did you know that your dad had another family."

"No. There's no way."

"But some of us formed shadow families of our own, after all. We boarded buses, crossed whole continents on trains, or watched the lights of our old cities shrink as we climbed into the sky."

Mia Alvar, "Shadow Families"

Thank You

To the hardworking, intrepid folks at Timeless, Infinite Light who make me and this work feel so seen: Emji Spero, Ted Rees, Zoe Tuck, Joel Gregory, Lauren Levin, Gabriel Ojeda-Sague, Andrea Abi-Karam, Jasmine Gibson.

To mentors who have helped me make my writing a brave space for grieving: Mady Schutzman (for encouraging me to be accountable by sending her work every day for a few days to get me started), Janet Sarbanes, Jen Hofer, M. NourbeSe Philip and Doug Kearney. I appreciate those who were in Jen Hofer's Poetics of Translation course in Fall 2011 at CalArts. You helped this work in its earliest stages.

For my family; for my Sapigao, Lobo, Sabio, and Cabiles families. This book is one quadrant on a map of who we are. Thanks, to Ma, for telling me about the tapes and letting me listen to them. To my Dad, for leaving them behind for me to find; this is how you have been able to teach me in your absence. To my brother, William, for whom this story would not exist without. Thank you to my step-dad, who is here, too. And always love to Paolo, for supporting me throughout this process.

To the friends who've helped me pull through this particular story and all of its forms: Grace Burns, Bel Poblador, Shana Mirambeau, Kirstie Mah, for answering your phones and/or calling me back when I called to weep or not. To Ebony Williams, Sonal Malkani, Melissa R. Sipin, Neni Demetriou, Nijla Mu'min, K. Bradford, Jessica Felleman, Lianna Kissinger-Virizlay (our talks about fathers stay with me), Cynthia Yee, April Pablo, Caz Salamanca, Paola Rodelas, Lorenz Dumuk, Ngoho Reavey, Jessi Sabogal, Denise Benavides, Stephanie Sajor, Eddy M. Gana, Jr., and to Jay Santa Cruz who pushed and validated this work into its final shape. To Michelle Lin and Kazumi Chin for our first book blues talks. To Kundiman & VONA all day. Thank you to Jeremy Keith Villaluz and Terisa Siagatonu for blurbing the chapbook. Thank you to Cathy Linh Che, Eleni Sikelianos, and Jason Magabo Perez, whose works have influenced and blessed this book.

For April, Auntie Fely, Ninang Rosal & family; to Nate Nevado and the Nevado family; to Mel Espineuva+Aure and family; to the Du-muk family; to Uncle Julius, Jordan, and Jucel—Auntie Jocie once shared one of my poems on Facebook—and I miss her magandang smile. Grieving/healing is a long, worthy road, and I am so sorry for your losses.

Robin Park and Tammy Byrnes, whose Angel Card readings connected me to my family and my purpose.

To Arturo "Al" Garcia who taught me all of these Ilokano words and put up with my bastos nature. To Jake de Grazia and Lauren M. Whaley for documenting this story back in 2012, and to Tom Dibblee for connecting us.

Thank you, Luther Vandross and Tamyra Gray, for singing your shattering versions of a song I'd play that would never ever end / how I'd love love love / to dance with my father again.

And to Frank Ocean's "Self-Control." This song is everything to me.

Thank the earth for amethyst, black tourmaline, rose quartz, quartz, and pyrite.

Acknowledgements

A chapbook of this work *you don't know what you don't know* was edited by Amy Berkowitz for Mondo Bummer Books in Fall 2017.

"Contrastify" and "Apostrophize" were published in *Underblong* Journal by editors Chen Chen and Sam Wein in Summer 2017.

"Where My Name is From" was published in *Namjai: A Tribute Anthology of Bay Area Asian Pacific Islander Poets vol. 1* by The Re-Write in winter 2013. But most of you have seen it on YouTube. Thank you to Lorenz Dumuk for soliciting this work.

Sections from this book have also been published in *TAGVVERK* by editor Steven Perez, *agape* literary journal by editors Taylor McDaniel and Sean Pessin, and Waxwing by editors W. Todd Kaneko and Justin Bigos.